Elizabeth,

thought you would like
this book.

Mary L Andrew

# THE
# WISDOM AND PRAYERS
# OF THE POPE

# THE
# WISDOM AND PRAYERS
## OF
# POPE
## THE

## REFLECTIONS AND GUIDANCE FROM BENEDICT XVI

**INTRODUCTION BY** Ruth Rees

**About Ruth Rees**: Over the years, Londoner Ruth Rees has worked as a journalist and a public relations consultant in Britain, Spain, South Africa and Switzerland. She has written on numerous subjects for the *Spectator*, the *Daily Mail* and many overseas publications.

Her book *The Rosary in Space and Time* was published in the UK, USA, Poland and Colombia. In 2006, Ruth won two international journalism awards; from the Costa del Sol and from Gibraltar.

**Picture credits**: Bridgeman Art Library 13, 25; Corbis 2, 3, 4, 5, 10, 20, 27, 31, 37, 42, 48, 61, 63; Rex Features 46, 53; Shutterstock 16, 39, 50–1, 58–9. Front cover image © Photo Service – L'Osservatore Romano 2010.

ARCTURUS

This edition published in 2010 by Arcturus Publishing Limited
26/27 Bickels Yard, 151–153 Bermondsey Street,
London SE1 3HA

Copyright © 2010 Arcturus Publishing Limited

Copyright of extracts by Benedict XVI © 2010 Libreria Editrice Vaticana, Vatican City.

All rights reserved. No part of this publication may be reproduced, stored in a retrieval system, or transmitted, in any form or by any means, electronic, mechanical, photocopying, recording or otherwise, without written permission in accordance with the provisions of the Copyright Act 1956 (as amended). Any person or persons who do any unauthorised act in relation to this publication may be liable to criminal prosecution and civil claims for damages.

ISBN: 978-1-84837-719-6
AD001605EN

Printed in China

# Contents

# Introduction

One day, Jesus asked his little band of disciples what people were saying about him and who they thought he was. They gave various replies, but only Simon the fisherman gave the right reply: 'Thou art the Christ, the Son of the Living God'. And Jesus said, 'Blessed are you, Simon son of Jona, for flesh and blood has not revealed this to you, but my father who is in heaven, and I tell you, you are Peter, and on this rock I will build my church and the powers of death shall not prevail against it, I will give you the keys of the kingdom of heaven and whatever you bind on earth shall be bound in heaven, and whatever you loose on earth shall be loosed in heaven.' [Matthew 16:16-17] By these words, Simon became Peter (the name was a play on the Greek word for rock) and the world's first Pope.

As the papal line continues

over the centuries, each Holy Father has had to deal with the problems of his own era, and remarkably, even though in the distant past some Popes led scandalous lives, none tampered with Catholic doctrine which remained – and remains to this day – unchanged.

In more modern times the Church has been blessed by exceptional Pontiffs, but when John Paul II died his successor would have to face a world more complex and full of challenges than ever before. So who would be chosen as the right man for our difficult era?

Following the death of a Pope, a conclave is called, summoning the world's Cardinals who are under 80 years of age to come to Rome for a papal election. The coordination of such an event would be challenging even for the most experienced congress and events organizers, but the Vatican has had centuries of experience and the entire operation swung into immediate action under the management of the Dean of the College of Cardinals, whose job it is to call the Conclave when a new Pope has to be elected. In 2005, the Dean was in fact Cardinal Joseph Ratzinger, who was also the Prefect of the Congregation for the Doctrine of the Faith, in charge of the Curia whose officials help the Pope to run the Church.

One hundred and fifteen Cardinals took part in the election, while outside, excited crowds – Romans and visitors from many countries – waited to hear who would be the next Holy Father. When there isn't a clear result the voting papers are burned together with some wet hay that blackens the smoke as it curls up from the chimney of the Sistine Chapel. Sometimes, the process can go for several days until there is a clear majority, but happily, in the 2005

election, the result was swift. White smoke poured out of the chimney and the crowds cheered with delight when the new Pope came out onto the balcony and blessed them. Cardinal Joseph Ratzinger had been elected 265th Pope of the Catholic Church – the Holy Father of the world's 1.4 billion Catholics.

It is the custom for a newly elected Pope to chose a name by which he will be known for the rest of his life, and the former Cardinal Ratzinger chose that of Benedict – after both the 6th-century Saint Benedict of Nursia and Benedict XV, a Pope who suffered greatly because his pontificate coincided with the terrible years of the First World War (1914–18), when millions of young Christians on both sides had fought each other and died in the squalor of the trenches. With this in mind, the new Benedict XVI would place the

message of peace at the heart of his pontificate.

Joseph Ratzinger was born in 1927 in a beautiful rural region of Bavaria where 70% of the people were Catholics. When the Nazis came into power they not only slaughtered the Jewish population, but also targeted Christian traditions and beliefs. They closed monasteries, established euthanasia and banned crucifixes in schools.

Ordained priest in 1952, his character, deep faith and towering intellect resulted in his being well known and respected not just in Rome but also in the academic world. He became Archbishop of Munich in 1977, and later he was appointed to other key positions in Rome. People who have met him speak warmly of his gentle, unassuming manner and friendliness. There is a charming story that while he was still Cardinal Ratzinger, he would go out every day to feed a group of

stray cats who roamed around the district where he lived at the time. Undoubtedly he would have made other arrangements for them once he was living in the Vatican!

Pope Benedict XVI has specific ideas he wants to pursue during his pontificate, such as a search for unity with the churches of the East. Already, the relationship with the Orthodox churches is better now than in recent centuries.

Another aim is to create a structure to allow the Anglican community to enter into communion with the Catholic Church – the most important development since the Second Vatican Council of the 1960s.

His renewal of the Catholic liturgy is inspired by his desire to promote continuity with the traditions of the past while taking full advantage of more recent developments. In 2007, a great deal of goodwill was engendered when he gave his permission for the celebration of the Latin Mass as it was before the Second Vatican Council, for those people who prefer this form of the liturgy.

On a more general note, Pope Benedict XVI has denounced the culture of consumerism that has undermined traditional values and led to great inequalities across the world. He advocates a spiritual renewal and the development of a human community 'to encourage every People to share the needs of other Peoples, placing in common the goods of the earth that the Creator has destined for the entire human family' (see page 57).

Many readers of this excellent little book may already know a great deal about Benedict XVI and his theology; for others, it provides the opportunity to learn something about the inner thoughts and character of one of the greatest religious leaders of our time.

*Ruth Rees*

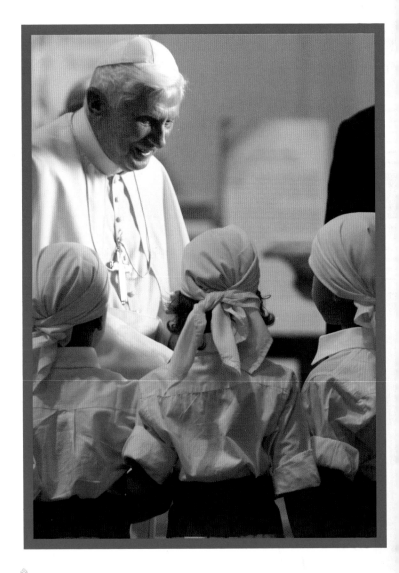

# Youth
## and the
# Family

'Many people say that children are capricious, that they are never happy with anything, that they consume toys, one after another, without being satisfied by them. You, on the other hand, say to Jesus: You are enough for me! Which means: you are our dearest friend who keeps us company when we play and when we go to school, when we are at home with our parents, our grandparents, our little brothers and sisters, and when we go out with our friends. You open our eyes so that we notice our sad companions and the many children in the world who are suffering hunger, illness and war. You are enough for us, Lord Jesus, you give us true joy, the joy that does not end like our games but is poured out into our souls and makes us good.'

'…why is it beautiful to be young? What is the reason for the dream of eternal youth? It seems to me that there are two crucial elements: youth still has the whole future before it. Everything is in the future, a time of hope. The future is full of promises. To be sincere, we must say that for many people the future is also dark, full of threats. One wonders: will I find a job? Will I find somewhere to live? Will I find love? What will my true future be? And in the face of these threats, the future can also appear as a great void. Today, therefore, many desire to stop time for fear of a future in emptiness. They want to enjoy all the beauties of life instantly – and in this way the oil in the lamp is consumed just as life is beginning. Thus it is important to choose the true promises that pave the way to the future, even with sacrifices. Those who have chosen God still have before them in old age a future without end and without threats.'

'How is it possible not to recall Jesus' special love for children? He wanted them beside him, he pointed them out to the Apostles as models to follow in their spontaneous, generous faith, in their innocence. With harsh words he warned people against despising or shocking them.'

'The process of globalization taking place in the world entails a need for mobility that obliges numerous young people to emigrate and live far from their home countries and their families. This brings about an unsettling feeling of insecurity that undoubtedly has repercussions on their ability to not only dream and build up a project for the future, but even to commit themselves to matrimony and start a family. These are complex and delicate questions that must be faced in due course, keeping in mind the reality of our times while referring to the social doctrine of the Church.'

'If you are engaged to be married, God has a project of love for your future as a couple and as a family. Therefore, it is essential that you discover it with the help of the Church, free from the common prejudice that says that Christianity with its commandments and prohibitions places obstacles to the joy of love and impedes you from fully enjoying the happiness that a man and woman seek in their reciprocal love. The love of a man and woman is at the origin of the human family and the couple formed by a man and a woman has its foundation in God's original plan [*see* Genesis 2:18-25]. Learning to love each other as a couple is a wonderful journey, yet it requires a demanding "apprenticeship". The period of engagement, very necessary in order to form a couple, is a time of expectation and preparation that needs to be lived in purity of gesture and words. It allows you to mature in love, in concern and in attention for each other; it helps you to practise self-control and to develop your respect for each other.'

'One of the challenges for our contemporaries, and in particular for youth, consists in not accepting to live merely in exteriority, in appearance, but in the development of the interior life, the unifying environment of being and acting, the place of recognizing our dignity as sons and daughters of God called to freedom, not separating ourselves from the font of life but remaining connected to it.'

'The Lord calls each of us by name, and entrusts to us
a specific mission in the Church and in society...
Consider seriously the divine call to raise a Christian
family, and let your youth be the time in which
to build your future with a sense of responsibility.
Society needs Christian families, saintly families!'

'...in a healthy family life we experience some of
the fundamental elements of peace: justice and love
between brothers and sisters, the role of authority
expressed by parents, loving concern for the members
who are weaker because of youth, sickness or old age,
mutual help in the necessities of life, readiness
to accept others and, if necessary, to forgive them.
For this reason, the family is the first and indispensable
teacher of peace.'

'Joseph was the model of a "just" man [Matthew 1:19]
who, in perfect harmony with his wife, welcomed the
Son of God made man and watched over his
human growth.'

'For believers, the family, the cell of communion on which society is founded, resembles a "domestic church in miniature" called to reveal God's love to the world. Dear brothers and sisters, help families to be a visible sign of this truth, to defend the values inscribed in human nature itself, and therefore common to all humanity, that is: life, the family and education.'

'The causes that lead to such painful decisions as abortion are of course many and complex. If, on the one hand, faithful to her Lord's commandment, the Church never tires of reaffirming that the sacred value of every human being's life originates in the Creator's plan, on the other hand, she encourages the promotion of every initiative in support of women and families in order to create the favourable conditions in which to welcome life, and the protection of the family institution founded on the marriage between a man and a woman. Not only has permitting recourse to the termination of pregnancy not solved the problems that afflict many women and a fair number of families, but it has also made another wound in our society, unfortunately, already burdened by deep suffering.'

# Celebrations and Events

## CHRISTMAS

'As we prepare to celebrate the Saviour's Birth joyfully in our families and our Ecclesial Communities, while a certain modern, consumerist culture tends to do away with the Christian symbols of the celebration of Christmas, may it be everyone's task to grasp the value of the Christmas traditions that are part of the patrimony of our faith and our culture, in order to pass them on to the young generations.

Let us remember in particular, as we look at the streets and squares of the cities decorated with dazzling lights, that these lights refer us to another light, invisible to the eyes but not to the heart. While we admire them, while we light the candles in churches or the illuminations of the crib and the Christmas tree in our homes, may our souls be open to the true spiritual light brought to all people of good will. The God-with-us, born in Bethlehem of the Virgin Mary, is the Star of our lives!'

'At Christmas we contemplate God made man,
divine glory hidden beneath the poverty of a Child
wrapped in swaddling clothes and laid in a manger;
the Creator of the Universe reduced to the helplessness
of an infant. Once we accept this paradox, we discover
the Truth that sets us free and the Love that transforms
our lives. On Bethlehem Night, the Redeemer becomes
one of us, our companion along the precarious paths
of history. Let us take the hand which he stretches out
to us: it is a hand which seeks to take nothing from us,
but only to give.'

'Wherever the dignity and rights of the human person
are trampled upon; wherever the selfishness of
individuals and groups prevails over the common good;
wherever fratricidal hatred and the exploitation of
man by man risk being taken for granted; wherever
internecine conflicts divide ethnic and social groups
and disrupt peaceful coexistence; wherever terrorism
continues to strike; wherever the basics needed for
survival are lacking; wherever an increasingly uncertain
future is regarded with apprehension, even in affluent
nations: in each of these places may the
Light of Christmas shine forth…'

'Christmas is appropriately emphasized by the many gifts that people give to one another in these days. But it is important that the principal Gift of which all other gifts are a symbol not be forgotten. Christmas is the day on which God gave himself to humanity, and in the Eucharist this gift of his becomes, so to speak, perfect.'

'The light of that first Christmas was like a fire kindled in the night. All about there was darkness, while in the cave there shone the true light "that enlightens every man" [John 1:9]. And yet all this took place in simplicity and hiddenness, in the way that God works in all of salvation history. God loves to light little lights, so as then to illuminate vast spaces. Truth, and Love, which are its content, are kindled wherever the light is welcomed; they then radiate in concentric circles, as if by contact, in the hearts and minds of all those who, by opening themselves freely to its splendour, themselves become sources of light.'

## LENT

'In our own day, fasting seems to have lost something
of its spiritual meaning, and has taken on,
in a culture characterized by the search for material
well-being, a therapeutic value for the care of one's
body. Fasting certainly bring benefits to physical
well-being, but for believers, it is, in the first place,
a "therapy" to heal all that prevents them from
conformity to the will of God.'

## EASTER

'"Behold, I will open your graves, and raise you from your graves, O my people; and I will bring you home into the land of Israel" [Ezekiel 37:12]. These prophetic words take on a singular value on Easter Day, because today the Creator's promise is fulfilled; today, even in this modern age marked by anxiety and uncertainty, we relive the event of the Resurrection, which changed the face of our life and changed the history of humanity. From the risen Christ, all those who are still oppressed by chains of suffering and death look for hope, sometimes even without knowing it.'

'The astonishing event of the resurrection of Jesus
is essentially an event of love: the Father's love
in handing over his Son for the salvation of the world;
the Son's love in abandoning himself to the Father's
will for us all; the Spirit's love in raising Jesus from the
dead in his transfigured body.'

'One of the questions that most preoccupies men
and women is this: what is there after death?
To this mystery today's solemnity allows us to respond
that death does not have the last word, because
Life will be victorious at the end. This certainty of ours
is based not on simple human reasoning, but on
a historical fact of faith: Jesus Christ, crucified and
buried, is risen with his glorified body. Jesus is risen
so that we too, believing in him, may have eternal life.
This proclamation is at the heart of the
Gospel message.'

# PASSOVER

'Because of that growth in trust and friendship, Christians and Jews can rejoice together in the deep spiritual ethos of the Passover, a memorial (*zikkarôn*) of freedom and redemption. Each year, when we listen to the Passover story we return to that blessed night of liberation. This holy time of the year should be a call to both our communities to pursue justice, mercy, solidarity with the stranger in the land, with the widow and orphan, as Moses commanded: "But you shall remember that you were a slave in Egypt and the Lord your God redeemed you from there; therefore I command you to do this" [Deuteronomy 24:18].'

*From a message to the Jewish Community
on the Feast of Pesah*

# *Peace*

## REFLECTION ON THE NAME CHOSEN: BENEDICT XVI

'At this first Meeting, I would like to begin by reflecting on the name that I chose on becoming Bishop of Rome and universal Pastor of the Church. I wanted to be called Benedict XVI in order to create a spiritual bond with Benedict XV, who steered the Church through the period of turmoil caused by the First World War. He was a courageous and authentic prophet of peace and strove with brave courage first of all to avert the tragedy of the war and then to limit its harmful consequences. Treading in his footsteps, I would like to place my ministry at the service of reconciliation and harmony between persons and peoples, since I am profoundly convinced that the great good of peace is first and foremost a gift of God, a precious but unfortunately fragile gift to pray for, safeguard and build up, day after day, with the help of all.'

'A united humanity will be able to confront the many
troubling problems of the present time: from
the menace of terrorism to the humiliating poverty
in which millions of human beings live, from the
proliferation of weapons to the pandemics and the
environmental destruction which threaten the future
of our planet.'

'We need to regain an awareness that we share a common destiny which is ultimately transcendent, so as to maximize our historical and cultural differences, not in opposition to, but in cooperation with, people belonging to other cultures. These simple truths are what make peace possible; they are easily understood whenever we listen to our own hearts with pure intentions. Peace thus comes to be seen in a new light: not as the mere absence of war, but as a harmonious coexistence of individual citizens within a society governed by justice, one in which the good is also achieved, to the extent possible, for each of them. The truth of peace calls upon everyone to cultivate productive and sincere relationships; it encourages them to seek out and to follow the paths of forgiveness and reconciliation, to be transparent in their dealings with others, and to be faithful to their word.'

'...*peace is both gift and task*. If it is true that peace between individuals and peoples – the ability to live together and to build relationships of justice and solidarity – calls for unfailing commitment on our part, it is also true, and indeed more so, that *peace is a gift from God.*'

The end of the Cold War 'was a moment when the widespread hope for peace induced many people to dream of a different world, where relations between peoples would develop, safe from the nightmare of war, and where the "globalization" process would unfold under the banner of a peaceful encounter of peoples and cultures in the context of a common international law inspired by respect for the needs of truth, justice and solidarity.

Unfortunately, this dream of peace never came true. On the contrary, the third millennium opened with scenes of terrorism and violence that show no sign of abating. Then, the fact that armed conflicts are taking place today against a background of the geographical and political tensions that exist in many regions may give the impression that not only cultural diversity but also religious differences are causes of instability or threats to the prospect of peace.

It is under this profile that the initiative John Paul II promoted 20 years ago has acquired the features of an accurate prophecy. His invitation to the world's religious leaders to bear a unanimous witness to peace serves to explain with no possibility of confusion that *religion must be a herald of peace.*'

'God of peace, bring your peace to our violent world:
peace in the hearts of all men and women
and peace among the nations of the earth.
Turn to your way of love
those whose hearts and minds
are consumed with hatred.

God of understanding,
overwhelmed by the magnitude of this tragedy,
we seek your light and guidance
as we confront such terrible events.
Grant that those whose lives were spared
may live so that the lives lost here
may not have been lost in vain.
Comfort and console us,
strengthen us in hope,
and give us the wisdom and courage
to work tirelessly for a world
where true peace and love reign
among nations and in the hearts of all.'

*From a Prayer at Ground Zero, New York*

'Pope John Paul II came here as a son of the Polish
people. I come here today as a son of the German
people. For this very reason, I can and must echo his
words: I could not fail to come here. I had to come.
It is a duty before the truth and the just due of all who
suffered here, a duty before God, for me to come here…
I have come here today: to implore the grace of
reconciliation – first of all from God, who alone can
open and purify our hearts, from the men and women
who suffered here, and finally the grace of
reconciliation for all those who, at this hour of our
history, are suffering in new ways from the power
of hatred and the violence which hatred spawns…
there is hope that this place of horror will gradually
become a place for constructive thinking, and that
remembrance will foster resistance to evil and
the triumph of love.'

*Address on a visit to the*
*Auschwitz Concentration Camp*

'In today's globalized world, it is increasingly evident
that peace can be built only if everyone is assured
the possibility of reasonable growth: sooner or later,
the distortions produced by unjust systems have to be
paid for by everyone. It is utterly foolish to build
a luxury home in the midst of desert or decay.
Globalization on its own is incapable of building peace,
and in many cases, it actually creates divisions
and conflicts.'

# Faith and Prayer

'God is always with us. Even in the darkest nights of our lives, he does not abandon us. Even in the most difficult moments, he remains present. And even in the last night, in the last loneliness in which no one can accompany us, the night of death, the Lord does not abandon us.

He is with us even in this final solitude of the night of death. And we Christians can therefore be confident: we are never left on our own. God's goodness is always with us.'

'Those who listen to the word of God and refer to it always, are constructing their existence on solid foundations. "Everyone then who hears these words of mine and acts on them," Jesus said, "will be like a wise man who built his house on rock" [Matthew 7:24]. It will not collapse when bad weather comes.'

'Clement Virgin, Mother of humanity,
turn your gaze to
the men and women of our time,
to peoples and to those
who govern them,
to nations and to continents;
comfort those who weep, who suffer,
who struggle because of
human injustice; sustain those
who waver under the weight of effort
and who look at the future
without hope; encourage those
who work to build a better world
where justice triumphs
and brotherhood
reigns, where selfishness,
hate and violence cease.
May every form and
manifestation of violence
be conquered by the
peace-making power
of Christ.'

'The recitation of the Rosary can help you learn the art
of prayer with Mary's simplicity and depth.
It is important that you make participation in the
Eucharist, in which Jesus gives himself for us, the heart
of your life. He who died for the sins of all desires
to enter into communion with each one of you and
is knocking at the doors of your hearts to give you
his grace.'

'In the millennium just past, and especially in the last centuries, immense progress was made in the areas of technology and science. Today we can dispose of vast material resources. But the men and women in our technological age risk becoming victims of their own intellectual and technical achievements, ending up in spiritual barrenness and emptiness of heart. That is why it is so important for us to open our minds and hearts to the Birth of Christ, this event of salvation which can give new hope to the life of each human being.'

'May the candle that you hold alight in your hands be for you, dear brothers and sisters, the sign of a sincere desire to walk with Jesus, refulgence of peace, who shines in the darkness and urges us in our turn to be light and support for those near to us.

May no one, especially those who find themselves in the difficult situation of suffering, feel alone and abandoned.'

*Holy Mass for the Sick*
*on the Feast of our Lady of Lourdes*

'God of all the ages,

on my visit to Jerusalem, the "City of Peace",

spiritual home to Jews, Christians and Muslims alike,

I bring before you the joys, the hopes and the aspirations,

the trials, the suffering and the pain of all your people

throughout the world.


God of Abraham, Isaac and Jacob,

hear the cry of the afflicted, the fearful, the bereft;

send your peace upon this Holy Land, upon the Middle East,

upon the entire human family;

stir the hearts of all who call upon your name,

to walk humbly in the path of justice and compassion.


"The Lord is good to those who wait for him,

to the soul that seeks him" [Lamentations 3:25]!'


*Prayer at the Western wall, Jerusalem*

'Humanly speaking, the word, my human word,
is almost nothing in reality, a breath. As soon as it is
pronounced it disappears. It seems to be nothing.
But already the human word has incredible power.
Words create history, words form thoughts,
the thoughts that create the word. It is the word
that forms history, reality.

Furthermore, the Word of God is the foundation
of everything, it is the true reality…
Let us pray to the Lord that he may help us search
the word, not only with our intellect but also with
our entire existence.'

# *Society* and *Environment*

'Questions on the immensity of the universe, its origins
and its end, as well as on understanding it, do not admit of
a scientific answer alone. Those who look at the cosmos, following
Galileo's lesson, will not be able to stop at merely what is observed
with the telescope; they will be impelled to go beyond it and
wonder about the meaning and end to which all creation is
ordered. At this stage philosophy and theology have an important
role in smoothing out the way towards further knowledge.
Philosophy, confronting the phenomena and beauty of creation,
seeks with its reasoning to understand the nature and finality
of the cosmos. Theology, founded on the revealed word,
examines the beauty and wisdom of the love of God who has left
his imprint on created nature.'

'The contribution of scientists is of primary importance. Together with the progress of our capacity to dominate nature, scientists must also contribute to help understand the depth of our responsibility for man and for nature entrusted to him.

On this basis it is possible to develop a fruitful dialogue between believers and non-believers; between theologians, philosophers, jurists and scientists, which can offer to legislation as well precious material for personal and social life.'

'In a spirit of collaboration, drawing on ancient wisdom, inspired by the Gospel, the Catholic Church makes a firm and heartfelt appeal that is very relevant for those participating in the Summit: "Give to eat to the one who is starving of hunger, because, if you do not give to him to eat, you will kill him" [*Decretum Gratiani*, c. 21, d. LXXXVI]. I assure you that, along this path, you can count on the support of the Holy See. Although it differentiates itself from States, it is united to their most noble objectives to seal a commitment that, by her nature, involves the entire international community: to encourage every People to share the needs of other Peoples, placing in common the goods of the earth that the Creator has destined for the entire human family.'

*Message to participants attending the*
*High-level Conference on World Food Security:*
*the Challenges of Climate Change and Bioenergy*

'Honest and straightforward relationships need to be promoted between individual persons and between peoples, thus enabling everyone to cooperate on a just and equal footing. Efforts must also be made to ensure *a prudent use of resources* and an *equitable distribution of wealth*. In particular, the aid given to poor countries must be guided by sound economic principles, avoiding forms of waste associated principally with the maintenance of expensive bureaucracies. Due account must also be taken of the moral obligation to ensure that the economy is not governed solely by the ruthless laws of instant profit, which can prove inhumane.'

'Biblical Revelation made us see that nature is a gift of the Creator, who gave it an inbuilt order and enabled man to draw from it the principles needed to "till it and keep it" [Genesis 2:15]. Everything that exists belongs to God, who has entrusted it to man, albeit not for his arbitrary use. Once man, instead of acting as God's co-worker, sets himself up in place of God, he ends up provoking a rebellion on the part of nature, "which is more tyrannized than governed by him" [citation from *John Paul II, Encyclical Letter*]. Man thus has a duty to exercise responsible stewardship over creation, to care for it and to cultivate it.'

## ON AMERICA

'From the dawn of the Republic, America's quest
for freedom has been guided by the conviction
that the principles governing political and social life
are intimately linked to a moral order based on the
dominion of God the Creator. The framers of this
nation's founding documents drew upon this
conviction when they proclaimed the "self-evident
truth" that all men are created equal and endowed
with inalienable rights grounded in the laws of nature
and of nature's God. The course of American history
demonstrates the difficulties, the struggles, and the
great intellectual and moral resolve which were
demanded to shape a society which faithfully embodied
these noble principles.'

*Welcoming Ceremony Address at The White House*

# ON EUROPE

'For many years Europe has been aware of its essential cultural unity, despite the constellation of national cultures that shaped its countenance. It is good to emphasize that contemporary Europe, which begins its venture into the Third Millennium, is the product of two millennia of civilization.

It is deeply rooted in the large and ancient patrimony of Athens and Rome and in the fertile terrain of Christianity, which proved capable of creating new cultural heritages while at the same time receiving the original contribution of every civilization. The new humanism that emerged from the dissemination of the Gospel message exalts all the elements worthy of the human person and of his transcendent vocation, purifying them from the dross that obscures the authentic face of man created in the image and likeness of God. Thus Europe today appears to us as a precious cloth whose fabric is woven from the principles and values spun from the Gospel, while the national cultures have been able to embroider it with an immense variety of perspectives that express the religious, intellectual, technical, scientific and artistic abilities of the *Homo europeus*. In this sense, we may affirm that Europe has had and still has a cultural influence on the entire human race, and cannot fail to feel particularly responsible not only for its own future but also for the future of humanity as a whole.'

62

## ON LATIN AMERICA

'In this geographical area, Catholics are in the majority. This means that they must make a particular contribution to the common good of the nation. The word solidarity will acquire its full meaning when the living forces of society, each in its own sphere, commit themselves seriously to building a future of peace and hope for all… I am happy to be able to spend some days among the Brazilian people. I am well aware that the soul of this people, as of all Latin America, safeguards values that are radically Christian, which will never be eradicated.'

*Welcome Ceremony; Apostolic journey to Brazil*

# SOURCES OF WISDOM AND PRAYERS